DO NOT SETTLE FOR LESS
TURNING **MESS**
INTO
Success

A Guide to
Increased Productivity

JOHN AND
JACQUE EAVES, PHD

Turning Mess Into Success

John & Jacqueline Eaves
Fredericksburg, VA
www.yourultimatelifecoach.com

Library of Congress Cataloging-in-Publication Data

Eaves, John, 1973-
Eaves, Jacqueline, 1973-
     Do Not Settle For Less Turning Mess Into Success: A
Guide to Increased Productivity
     ISBN (pbk) 978-0-9884384-0-8
Authors photograph courtesy of Extending Time Photography
www.extendingtimephoto.com

DEDICATION

In Memory of our beloved Great-Grandparents &
Grandparents

Glenwood & Ethel Mae Eaves
Eddie & Bertha Jones
Charles & Naomi Norwood
Virgie Smith
Leroy & Imogene Williams

Thank you for your wisdom and instruction throughout the years. Although you are gone, we hold dearly your love and direction and strive to instill your teachings in the generations to come!

.

CONTENTS

ACKNOWLEDGMENTS

The God we serve is able to do exceedingly and abundantly more than we could ever ask or imagine according to the power that lives in us! Our God is a rewarder of them that diligently seek Him; this work is a testament to His love and those who have graciously poured into us over the years in expectation that we would walk in the promises God has for us!

To our grandmother Daisy M. Smith and our parents, Bishop Shirley Sanders, John Eaves, Sr. and Rev. J.J. & Terica Richardson, thank you for giving us life and instilling values, love, humility, and mercy as a roadmap of how to walk upright before man and God. You truly are our foundation and Godly examples!

Many spiritual parents and leaders guided our journey: Rev. Leonard B. Lacey and Dr. Renee Lacey; Bishop Courtney and Pastor Janeen McBath, Rev. James Miller; and Deacon Homer and Karen Wilson – Thank you for the spiritual seeds you planted in us! Some planted, some watered, but God gives the increase…your work has not been in vain; we thank you for your ministry and your unselfish sacrifice to do God's will!

To our children Janae and Joshua; we are excited about God's plan for your lives. Know that Mommy and Daddy love you; but Jesus loves you most! To all of our friends, family, co-laborers in Christ; thank you for your continued prayers and support. You give us strength to stay in the race – we love you all!

1

DO NOT SETTLE FOR LESS

"The biggest human temptation
is to settle for too little."
~ Thomas Merton

If you are like us, you may have spent a good part of your life striving for balance, education, and success. Our parents instilled within us early in life the importance of hard work, good work ethic, maintaining a good name, and total dependence on God.

These basic tenets have provided us the discipline and structure needed to graduate from high school and college, find one another as suitable companions, and begin the journey we call life, together as one.

We established early in our relationship that God is the center of our relationship and adopted what Mark 10:9 implores:

"Therefore what God has joined together, let no one separate."

Over time, we have grown and matured in our relationship and in our walk with God and determined that we will not settle for less than what God has predestined for us. Even with the best-laid plans, life happens and often becomes a little messy. A mess is described as disarray or as noted in Merriam-Webster "a disordered, untidy, offensive, or unpleasant state."

As a military family, we have endured several military moves. These moves often result in periods of disarray as we purge and discard things that we outgrew or no longer use. This process gets messy. Such is true in our lives.

As we grow and develop, there are things, people, and habits that must be released. The transition is laborious and time consuming, but remember: do not settle. Turn your mess into success!

Visualize the desired outcome as a destination worth achieving - a clean closet, renewed peace, increased productivity, or better utilization of your time, talents, and treasures. This book is a how-to guide to begin reflecting and exploring ways to turn your mess into success! Do not settle for less.

REFLECT

Reflect upon areas of your life that you consider are in a mess, disordered, untidy, or unpleasant state. Note particular areas of your life that you would like to improve.

Physically

Spiritually

Emotionally

Financially

Personally

EXPLORE

EPHESIANS 1:11, 12 (NIV)

"In him we were also chosen, having been predestined according to the plan of him who works out everything in conformity with the purpose of his will, in order that we, who were the first to put our hope in Christ, might be for the praise of his glory."

REFLECT & EXPLORE!

God has a purpose and plan for your life.

Ephesians 1:11,12 reflects several keys to your success. Reflect and explore the scripture to discover how to apply the principles to your life.

SUCCESS STRATEGY

My success is directly connected to God's plan and purpose for my life!

2
PRODUCTIVITY

"Never confuse motion with action."
~ Benjamin Franklin

Many individuals are extremely busy today; however, very few are productive from the standpoint of setting goals and implementing a course of action. The process of identifying goals and incorporating actions ensures authentic success in realizing and accomplishing goals and/or dreams.

Productivity is the ability to generate or bring forth goods and services with efficiency and measured results. Observable when examining the root cause of the non-productivity issue:

Imbalance of time management and God given gifts and talents.
Failure to visualize what constitutes success.

Unwillingness to give up hindrances in return for measureable success.

Success is the favorable or prosperous termination of attempts or endeavors. Note the key words: *attempts or endeavors*. Action is required.

Envision a bulls eye in the center of a target. As darts are hurled toward the center it is likely that some attempts may fall shy of the target, the measure of success. The darts represent attempts or endeavors. Each dart represents the possibility and opportunity to achieve the most desirous outcome. This is where productivity will have the greatest impact.

God has afforded each of us a portion of time, talents, and treasure. The question becomes how to balance the gifts and blessings of God for a more productive work in the Kingdom.

The predominant question for Christians when considering why we struggle with allocations of our time, talents, and our treasure is what the carnal nature (flesh) desires concerning these gifts versus the God's plan for our lives.

God gives every person a measure of gifts, talents, and treasures for the purpose of glorifying

Him and growing the Kingdom of God; therefore, when there is a struggle with how to best utilize these gifts, it is time to stop and reflect on purpose.

Was an opportunity missed to use the gifts, talents, or treasures? Remember the purpose of the gifts is not for personal gain, but for His plan of spreading the gospel around the world and throughout all ages. How do you know what to do?

The Bible is the guide for your success. Joshua 1:8 is loaded with daily principles to lead to your success: *"Keep this Book of the Law always on your lips; meditate on it day and night, so that you may be careful to do everything written in it. Then you will be prosperous and successful."*

Joshua had an enormous responsibility to lead and settle the children of Israel into Canaan. Like Joshua, once we began to incorporate saying the Word of God, meditating on it, and actually doing as it instructs did we begin to redefine our definition of success.

Once we were clear, we began to see progress toward our goals for *His* purpose. It has been a humbling experience. This meant that we had to stop looking at what the world views as success and begin to align our lives with what is written in the Word.

REFLECT

How are you utilizing the blessings of God for a more productive work in His Kingdom?

Success is:

Productivity is:

What areas of your life could benefit from increased productivity?

What is the root cause of your lack of productivity?
Imbalance of time management and God given gifts and talents.

Failure to visualize what constitutes success.

Unwillingness to give up hindrances in return for measureable success.

Others causes:

EXPLORE

JAMES 1:17 (NIV)

> *"Every good and perfect gift is from above, coming down from the Father of the Heavenly lights, who does not change life shifting shadows."*

REFLECT & EXPLORE

Your gifts are for expansion of God's Kingdom!

Reflect and explore James 1:17 to discover how to apply the principles to your life.

SUCCESS STRATEGY

Count your good and perfect gifts!

3

TIME

"There is a time for everything,
and a season for every activity
under the heavens."
Ecclesiastes 3:1 (NIV)

One of the main issues people face is how to manage time. The struggle with ineffective time management can lead to frustrations when unclear of the Creator's intent. Secondly, time management is increasingly complicated when there is failure to prioritize the events and responsibilities of our daily lives.

Consider the sinful nature of man and fleshly acts; not only is time for Kingdom-work a struggle, but talents and treasures for God's glory typically rank low in overall priorities.

The Bible highlights two different dimensions of time. The Greek word *"chronos"* is a span of time and *"kairos"* is a specific point of time. An example of *chronos* is the forty years the Israelites spent wondering in the wilderness; this dimension of time has a very specific start point and end point. An excellent example of *kairos* can be found in Mark's gospel: *"The time is fulfilled, and the Kingdom of God is at hand. Repent, and believe the gospel."* – Mark 1:15

Jesus Christ, our Lord and Savior chose a very specific and deliberate time to fulfill His plan of redemption and offered the gift of salvation to the world. Our lives on earth have a specific start and end point correlating with our birth and ending with our death.

Like our Savior, we also have a *kairos* moment in which we are to fulfill the purpose and destiny. He preordained for each and every Christian – those who have accepted Him as Lord and Savior.

The struggle often experienced with our *kairos* moment is that as descendents of Adam, mankind is born in sin and shaped in iniquity (Psalms 51:5). Therefore, the carnal nature wants to have control over every aspect of our lives including our time. We see this more clearly in the actual meaning of the word "flesh."

The Greek transliteration of flesh has two slightly different meanings:

> *olethros* means death, destruction, and ruin;
>
> *sarkikos* means having the nature of flesh, i.e. under the control of animal appetites governed by mere human nature; not by the Spirit of God.

Understanding the nature of flesh, its characteristics, and tendencies paints a broader picture of why Christians have struggles with their gifts that seem uncontrollable. When carnality has precedence over the order and direction of time, the destructive tendencies and animal instincts are powerful and overwhelming to the point where, if unchecked, they are granted full access to reign in all areas of our lives.

Leading researchers of effective time management have concluded that one of the top complaints received from respondents has to do with not enough hours in the day to complete all given tasks.

Time management requires realizing where time is lost and secondly, how to be more accountable for the time we have available. The focus becomes one of understanding the elements of time we have no control over and maximizing the elements of time we do have the ability to control.

Examples of time management and activities we must perform daily include: maintaining the body (sleep, cooking/eating, physical exercise), maintaining a home, driving to and from work, and just overall wait time from activities like standing in line at the bank and sitting in traffic for hours upon hours!

There are areas in our lives where we have considerable amounts of control, yet lack accountability. These unaccountable areas take range from procrastination, laziness, failing to prioritize significant events, and how to utilize our rest and down time. Consider at least one person in your life that can hold you accountable.

Accountability can be addressed through the carnal nature which suggests that our time can be better utilized doing other things which may include: focusing on career advancement; activities with friends and social groups, pursuing advanced degrees, television, entertainment, sporting and children activities. Do not forget, God has purposed a very specific plan and intent for each of our lives. It is in ultimately knowing His purpose and will for our lives that we will allocate our time to the things He has set.

Another issue Christians struggle with concerning time is simply not understanding or caring for the current season that they are living. We all seem to enjoy the fun seasons of life like teenage years, college, and dating periods with significant others. What happens when those seasons pass and we have to move into a more mature season of life?

1 Corinthians 13:11 states, *"When I was a child, I spoke as a child; I understood as a child, I thought as a child; but when I became a man, I put away childish things."*

There is a season for everything, but we must also recognize when that season has passed and embrace the new season and new things God is doing in our lives.

JACQUE'S
TESTIMONY
ON TIME

We enjoyed seven years of marriage before children. That was a wonderful season. We wanted to take time to establish our marriage, careers, and finances before planning to have children. We traveled, bought our first home, started two businesses, invested in real estate, and served in our local church. We felt we were in a good place and decided we were ready to grow our family. It was at that time we were faced with unforeseen fertility issues.

This period was stressful as I began to undergo fertility treatments. John was extremely supportive during this time, but traveled a lot. This complicated matters a bit as I underwent daily shots, weekly doctor's visits, and an ongoing emotional roller coaster. I recognized I was a mess!

I sought God for direction and acceptance for His will for my life. John and I began to pray together and seek God and He strengthened our marriage even more. During this time, I was a Clinician with a therapeutic foster care and in home counseling agency.

I loved providing therapeutic and clinical services to youth and families to ensure a stable home environment. I will never forget the day I was advised of a new client that was assigned to my caseload. She was a pregnant teenager. I struggled with understanding why this young lady was on my caseload and if I could actually assist her during this season in my life.

I prayed and asked God to guide me in counseling her. She debated her options and decided, with the support of her family to keep her child. I realized that I had a job to do and that God was in control of both of our lives. I accompanied her to doctor's appointments and considered it a blessing to see this young lady evolve from a scared, self-centered teen into a caring, loving mother.

As time went on, we were given orders to relocate. I was faced with the reality that we would terminate fertility treatments and pursue adoption once we settled into our new home.

During this period I had a dream and God showed me a beautiful baby girl and I rested in knowing that she would be born. I began looking in the children's section and even purchased an outfit and hung in the closet of what would be the nursery.

At that point of surrender, I understood clearly that God was in complete and total control of this area of our lives. One week after we completed our training to become foster adoptive parents we received the call that our daughter was born.

The adoption process took time, ongoing home visits and court hearings. We realized that God had placed our sweet, darling daughter in our care in *His* time! I am thankful that we were obedient and in place to receive her.

I will never forget the day I received the call to pick her up from the hospital. We had less than five hours to get everything needed to care for a newborn. John was able to leave work early to get a car seat and a few essentials.

Fortunately, John's sister was visiting and provided an extra set of hands to help us out. Friends and family stepped in and provided prayers and support to assist us with our beautiful blessing.

While this was not the plan we had to grow our family, it was indeed God's plan for us. We now have two beautiful children and I am passionate about increasing awareness of the need for foster adoptive homes for children and serve as a court appointed special advocate for children.

We now realize   through raising children and helping them realize the potential God preordained for them; we entered a new, albeit challenging season of our lives. We would not trade this season for anything in the world!

Through every season God wants to teach and mature us to walk in His purpose. In our season of child rearing God showed us how to prioritize and put others needs before our own. When it comes to time for the children, they are a top priority; ensuring they receive the care, love, and discipleship to be well equipped citizens of the Kingdom.

We can't answer for you, but think about the times in your life where God moved you into a different season to mature you and help you in prioritizing the things that matters most in your life.

For us, it was during those challenging seasons where we learned to trust God more on how we managed time and what we allowed to have priority in our lives. Trust God even more during your challenging seasons and He will direct your paths including how you manage your time.

What it all comes down to is a realization of whose time it really is! Here is a little secret: your time, your talents, and your treasure all belong to God!

Acts 17:24-25 tells us, *"God, who made the world and everything in it, since He is Lord of Heaven and earth, does not dwell in temples made with hands. Nor is He worshiped with men's hands, as though He needed anything, since He gives to all life, breath, and all things."*

This is very clear, God is the author, creator, and Lord over all things; also He is the giver of all things including your time, talent, and treasures!

Therefore, when God gives these gifts it is for His glory and His purpose. In Ephesians 5:15-17 Paul declares, *"See then that you walk circumspectly, not as fools but as wise, redeeming the time, because the days are evil. Therefore do not be unwise, but understand what the will of the Lord is."*

God wants us to be wise concerning how we use time and our gifts. There are all manner of obstacles to distract and deter us from the appointed course God has set. When we understand the will of God and his plan for our lives, we will glorify and honor his name because we are walking in the purpose He has established for us.

People oftentimes have problems grasping the blessings God purposed for them. Our God is so awesome; through His plan not only does he bless us with eternal life, he also gives us hundredfold blessing during this present time!

In Mark's gospel (Chapter 10:29-30), Jesus tells us: *"Assuredly, I say to you, there is not one who has house or brothers or sisters or father or mother or wife or children or lands, for my sake and the gospel's, who shall not receive a hundredfold now in this time--houses and brothers and sisters and mothers and children and lands, with persecutions--and in the age to come, eternal life."*

The word "assuredly" means you can count on it! Jesus wants you to put your time and top priority in things of the Kingdom, eternal life is a given and you shall receive a hundredfold blessings... now! God's Word is always true and He cannot lie, the problem is a lack of belief or lack of knowledge of the promises He has made.

We encourage you to study and learn more

of God's Word and His will for you. Don't miss the promises and blessings in His Word. We are all extremely important to God's Kingdom, so much that He called us joint-Heirs with Him!

Not only that, He tells us that suffering now does not compare to the glory which will be revealed in us. Allocate your time to the things which give God glory and you will be blessed immeasurably.

REFLECT

God created me for this purpose:

Reflect on your daily responsibilities and list them:

Think about daily activities that are time wasters:

EXPLORE

EPHESIANS 5:15-17 (NIV)

> *"Be very careful, then, how you live—not as unwise but as wise, making the most of every opportunity, because the days are evil. Therefore do not be foolish, but understand what the Lord's will is."*

REFLECT & EXPLORE

Your time, your talents, and your treasure all belongs to God!

Reflect and explore Ephesians 5:15-17 to discover how to apply the principles to your life.

There is no doubt that "the days are evil." There is no time for foolishness. Commit yourself to make sure that time is used wisely.

Ways to make good use of time:

SUCCESS STRATEGY
Study and understand what the Lord's will is!

4

TALENT

"When I stand before God
At the end of my life,
I hope that I would not
Have a single bit of talent left,
and could say,
'I used everything you gave me'."

~Erma Bombeck

Having a talent or several talents is a wonderful gift from God! We are to be a blessing to the Kingdom with the gifts He's deposited in us.

However, like any gift received; there is a struggle with how and for what purpose talents should be used. The fleshly nature suggests that talents are for personal gain and influence. The natural instincts of man will say: "I will develop this talent to make me rich" or "with this talent I will get the career I desire." Other struggles with talents include using them to gain influence or attention of certain groups; or using a talent as a source of validation among different crowds.

A talent is defined as a natural endowment or ability of superior quality. The Greek word for talent is *talanton* meaning measurement of gold or silver. Hence, we derive that a talent is something of value and significance. It is imperative our talents are not taken for granted.

Have you ever encountered a person with a great talent or ability that casually dismisses it as something he or she just picked up and didn't give much thought? Every good and perfect gift comes from God above (James 1:17) if He has not revealed your talents, pray for revelation and clarity of your gifts that you too will showcase for His glory.

God uses our talents collectively to build his Kingdom and we all are contributors! In the book of Exodus as the Israelites wondered in the wilderness for forty years God still desired to be close and dwell with them so He commanded a tabernacle built.

In chapter 31 of Exodus God gave superior talents to two men named Bezalel and Aholiab to construct the tabernacle according to the intricate specifications God had commanded. God commissioned these two brothers for a great work requiring specialized talent in order that His presence would be established for Israel during a time of struggle before entering the Promised Land.

It is important to note these men likely already had tremendous talent; after all, while slaves in Egypt Israelites were builders, masons, and skilled workers under Pharaoh.

We oftentimes miss the fact that people may have natural talents and God given abilities; however, it is important to recognize that skills are learned and improved over time.

When talents and skills are submitted to God's purpose that He anoints them along with others in the Kingdom to do a marvelous work where He can be glorified.

Throughout scripture we see that God works through multiplication. God wants to take the talents and gifts He has placed in us and multiply them exceedingly to accomplish His plan. We first see this in Genesis (chapter 1:28) where He told Adam and Eve to *"be fruitful and multiply; fill the earth and subdue it; have dominion over the fish of the sea...every living thing that moves on the earth."*

God wants to use your talents and skills further multiplying them for an output that elevates you to a place He predestined. Look at Abraham, out of the covenant between God and Abraham; He multiplied his seed into a great nation.

Multiplication is a great principle, through multiplication a small measure is compounded to a point where it is abundantly and exceedingly overflowing greater than something you ever hoped or imagined. Be encouraged, and know that your talents are for God's purpose and glory.

Out of your submission you will see Him link you with other vessels He has called unto His purpose and with God's anointing (that is the awesome power of God), you will see multiplication of your seed and your treasures which will simply blow your mind!

REFLECT

Talent- A natural endowment or ability of superior influence. My talents are:

Skill- A learned ability. My skills are:

EXPLORE
MATTHEW 25:29 (NIV)

"For whoever has will be given more, and they will have an abundance. Whoever does not have, even what they have will be taken from them."

REFLECT & EXPLORE

This is how I will use my talents and skills to glorify God:

SUCCESS STRATEGY

Submit your talents and skills to God's purpose and glorify Him!

5

TREASURE

"For where your treasure is,
there your heart will be also."
~ Matthew 6:21

The topic of treasure and how to utilize it in the Kingdom is often a touchy subject in church. First, there is a worldly perception of money and church often filled with negative images or thoughts of church leaders misusing church finances. Secondly, the carnal struggle within continually raises the question "why does the church need my money anyway?"

The paradigm shift for us happened when we began to see how God wanted to bless us out of obedience versus what the church leader's intent was with regard to monetary treasures.

In Luke's gospel (chapter 6:38) Jesus tells us to *"give and it will be given to you: good measure, pressed down, shaken together, and running over will be put into your bosom. For with the same measure that you use, it will be measured back to you."*

Two interesting points regarding this verse: it does not specifically say what to give. Naturally, the assumption is money, but it also applies to the other gifts and talents God has given. Whatever you place value on; give it.

Secondly, it does not say anything about giving to a church leader; it simply says to give and a good measure will be returned to you. When we examine the Word of God for ourselves we learn of His promises and blessings if we are obedient to His will.

Through God's word we learn the leader's intent doesn't matter; what matters is God looks at our heart and blesses us according to our obedience. Try God's word for yourself and observe the wonderful and amazing things He will do because of your obedience!

JOHN'S
TESTIMONY
ON TREASURE

Before I was faithful in my giving, I would Hear preachers quote Malachi 3:10, *'Bring all the tithes into the storehouse, that there may be food in my house, and try me now in this…,'* I would always think, "Food in your house; what about food in my house?"

God still had much work to do in me! But, that was a true representation of the struggle I was battling in my flesh. My flesh was saying, I have bills just like everyone else; and once I get caught up on all of my bills then I will be faithful in my giving.

The problem was I kept saying this for over 10 years; and it was not until I activated my faith and submitted my finances to God that I began to see the burden of debt diminish."

In the book of James (chapter 2:20) we find "… *faith without works is dead….*" It is through the elevation of faith that we begin to see things as God intended. The Bible tells us we are made in his image; therefore, if I am made like Him I am able to present some of the same qualities that He has.

We all have this ability, but it is through our communion with Him and knowledge of Him that we mature our spirit to the point that surpasses all struggles with the flesh. God is able to supply all your needs according to His riches and glory, so it is not a question of your need; because God is bigger than your need.

The question is your faith; do you believe you have the faith the size of a mustard seed that if you tell a mountain to be moved it shall be so (Matthew 17:20)? It is your faith in God and his promises that will remove your struggle on how to allocate your treasure. Decide now that you will not let the carnal nature choke out the plan of God for your life; feed your spirit with the word today.

Jesus tells us very clearly in Matthew's gospel (chapter 6 paraphrasing) that we are not to place our trust in treasures on earth because they will soon perish. Instead, put your treasure in Heavenly things where they cannot be lost or stolen because ultimately, where our treasure is our Hearts will be also. Therefore, it's not a question of the treasure itself because it is neither good nor evil; the question is the heart of an individual.

The man who has purposed in his heart to follow the will of God will make good on the promises of God and will accordingly be blessed out of the treasures He has stored up in the things of God.

Don't think for a moment God will bless evil deeds and things that do not bring Him glory. We see people all the time that seem to be blessed, but do not have the purposes of God in mind; you can rest assured, it will not last!

Jesus used the parable of talents to demonstrate to us what it means to use our time, talents, and treasures in the Kingdom of God for the purpose of the master. Found in Matthew's gospel (Chapter 25) the parable describes a man departing on a long journey, but prior to leaving gives talents to his servants. To one He gave five talents; to another he gave two talents; and to yet another he gave one talent.

This parable describes Jesus leaving for Heaven to prepare our place in eternity, but before He left He deposited gifts in us; His friends – those whom He is close to and have a relationship. This parable teaches us there is an expectation on the part of the Lord to use and multiply the gifts He left us. We see this because He rejoices with the servants who added to their talents and chastised the servant who hid his talent and did not receive a return.

The day is coming when we will all have to provide accountability on how we utilized the gifts the Lord has given us. We cannot afford to waste time letting the carnal nature rule our lives and the gifts God has given. We must be busy about our Father's business; uplifting his Kingdom and producing the expected return He seeks.

There is a critical element in understanding the parable of talents. Keep this though in mind when considering your talents - the servants who did well received more and the disobedient servant had his one talent taken away and given to the servants who had more.

What separated the servants who received more from the servant having his talent taken away centers on his lazy approach at handling the gift God gave Him. When we are lazy and procrastinate with regard to the things God blesses us to have, we place at jeopardy our gifts and not doing what God expects of us; that's a road we want to exit from quickly!

Never take for granted or be slack concerning God's gifts, but always seek to advance and multiply what He allocated so others will see the light in you and be drawn because you are the glory of God manifested in the earth and that may be the only light some will see.

From the parable of talents we see ourselves as God's chosen benefactors with an expectation to multiply what He has given; and having a realization there is an approaching day of accountability.

Your fleshly instincts will try to convince you to take shortcuts and put your gifts to work in areas that will bring self-glory and pride. Do not settle for less, you deserve success!

Start today by asking if you are truly walking in the love of Christ? The love of Christ constrains us to no longer live to ourselves, but to glorify the Redeemer.

When the Spirit of Christ lives within, is fed and elevated above the carnal instincts, it's no longer about self or mess. Adopt these principles and begin to walk in the image and purpose He has established.

His promises will ring true to bless a hundredfold in the present age and the age to come. He will turn your mess into success!

REFLECT

This is what I value:

As I reflect on my values, this is how I can display the love of Christ:

These are the resources God has given me to bless others:

EXPLORE

2 CORINTHIANS 9:6

"Remember this: Whoever sows sparingly will also reap sparingly, and whoever sows generously will also reap generously."

REFLECT & EXPLORE

Your gifts are for expansion of God's Kingdom!

Reflect and explore James 1:17 to discover how to apply the principles to your life.

SUCCESS STRATEGY

When I examine the Word of God for myself, I learn of His promises and blessings if I am obedient to His will!

DR. JACQUE'S TIPS TO INCREASED PRODUCTIVITY

Plan your day in advance!
> *Preferably the night before. Planning ahead helps to set priorities and measure daily outcomes.*

Limit your list to your top five priorities each day. *Items that are not completed can carry over to the next day.*

Be careful not to add too much to your day as it can become discouraging when you are unable to accomplish everything listed.

Use a list to ensure tasks are completed.
> *I live by a to do list. When it is not written down, it is easy to overlook critical items or spend time irrelevant things.*

Task lists assist in identifying and monitoring your daily, monthly and yearly goals.

There are great apps available to help in creating and maintaining to do lists. *I use Evernote, an app that is accessible from any laptop, tablet and/or cell phone. It has a ton of functions that I use for my business as well as my day-to-day tasks.*

Develop **SMART** goals, an ideal technique for short term and long term goals setting:
> **S**pecific
> **M**easureable
> **A**ttainable
> **R**ealistic
> **T**imely

When creating a goal be as Specific as possible. *Add as many details as possible.*

Ask yourself is the goal Measurable? *How will you gauge your progress?*

Is the goal Attainable? *How will you know when you have accomplished the goal?*

Is the goal Realistic? *Be true to yourself. This is*

your plan, be sure it is authentic.

Lastly, is the goal Timely? *Is it a sensible goal? Give it an end date.*

Try it out! Develop a SMART goal for each of the following areas of your life! Physical, Spiritual, Financial, Socially, Mental/ Personal/ Professional Development (see sample goal sheet.)

Share your goal with someone that will hold you accountable.

> *John and I have weekly accountability sessions. If there is a particular project or goal that we are tackling, we "touch base" and keep each other informed of progress or setbacks. This keeps the lines of communication of open.*

Use your time, talents and treasure for God's glory!

Which of these tips and strategies can you see yourself incorporating into your routine?

Do you have other tips that you use to increase productivity?   We would love to hear from you, share your tips on www.yulc.net

Do Not Settle For Less

Area of Life *Physical, Mental,* *Emotional, Social, or* *Spiritual*	Today's Date	Target Date	Date Completed

My SMART Goal

Specific: *This is exactly what I want to accomplish*

Measurable: *This is how I will know that I have accomplished my goal*

Attainable: *This is how this goal will be accomplished*

Relevant: *This goal is significant because:*

Time- Bound: *This goal will be achieved by*

This goal is important because:

The benefits of accomplishing this goal:

Affirmation toward this goal:

I will ask these people to help me:

This is how I will know that I have accomplished the goal:

Action Steps	Expected Completion Date	Date Completed

To book John & Jacque Eaves
to speak at your event or function,
please call
571.289.5159
www.johnandjacque.com

For coaching services visit us online:
www.yourultimatelifecoach.com